The Abou Abed Joke Book

كتاب نكات أبو عبد

Compiled by: Sabina Mahfoud
Illustrated by: Patrick Sfeir
Edited by: Hamad Haidar, Claude Karam, Faerlie Wilson
Designed by: Maya Tawil

turning**point**
B O O K S

15th Floor, Concorde Building, Dinan Street, Verdun, Beirut, Lebanon
P.O. Box: 14 - 6613
Tel: 00 961 1 752 100
Fax: 00 961 1 748 555
www.tpbooksonline.com

First edition, second print, May 2009

ISBN: 978-9953-0-0034-4

Printing:

To Abou Tara and Abou William

And as Abou Abed belongs to the Lebanese, part of the procceds from this book will be donated to the Lebanese non-profit organization CIFA to support sustainable development projects throughout Lebanon.

INTRODUCTION

Abou Abed, with his red *tarbouche* hat and considerable moustache (a symbol of his virility, no doubt), is one of the most recognizable comic characters in Lebanon. A figment of our imaginations, he has evolved to almost celebrity status and is at the center of an ever-growing number of jokes. He spends his time hanging out with his friend Abou Steif in a Beirut coffee shop where they play cards and backgammon. Over endless cups of tea, they tell each other far-fetched stories, usually orientated around their sexual potency. Not very well-off, he regularly tries his luck with card games and the lottery.

Abou Abed is married to Em Abed (literally, the mother of Abed) and has a son called, of course, Abed; they bear the brunt of his jokes - but sometimes manage to turn the tables back on him. We are always left guessing as to his profession and sexual orientation - he never seems to be working, and he is game for anything.

My fascination with Abou Abed began many years ago, during Lebanon's Civil War, when many of us were forced to stay close to home for long stretches of time. Evenings were spent with family and neighbors, telling Abou Abed jokes to forget the tensions; my husband is especially renowned for his incredible repertoire and elaborate renditions. A few years ago, I started to write down some of these jokes from memory, and the idea of publishing a book to introduce Lebanon's best-loved comic character to a wider audience came to mind.

Some of you are sure to dwell on my choice of jokes and may be disappointed about not seeing your favorite here. Those of you familiar with Abou Abed's character will know that some of his best stories are spicy and X-rated.

In my opinion, Abou Abed belongs to a utopian age when the average Lebanese had no real problems and all a man needed to worry about was how to have a good time with his friends. He represents the ordinary Lebanese guy, with all of his flaws, but also his greatness – in this case, an exceptional sense of humor. Although his stories cheer us up, I have often wondered how Abou Abed can get away with being such a chauvinist bigot – and still always come out on top, looking like a working-class hero!

So, where is he now? Abou Abed seems to be eternal and a survivor - he lives on with each and every generation in Lebanon. In terms of character, he may leave much to be desired - but as long as the jokes keep rolling in, who cares? Let's keep on searching, and let me know where you find him... I always love to hear his stories first-hand!

And last but not least, a big thanks to the incredibly talented Patrick who has brought Abou Abed to life and into the 21st century.

Sabina, Beirut, December 2008.
abou-abed@live.com

سأل أبو صطيف جارو أبو عبد
«عرفت شُو بدّك تجيب لأم عبد لعيد العشّاق؟»
ردّ أبو عبد «أكيد،
قالتلي إنّو بدّا شي فيه قلوب،
اشتريتلا ورق لعب».

At the coffeehouse one afternoon,
Abou Steif asked Abou Abed,
"So, have you figured out what you're going to get Em Abed for Valentine's Day?"
"Yes, I have," answered Abou Abed.
"She said she wanted something with hearts,
so I bought her a nice pack of cards."

على دق طاولة زهر، قال أبو عبد
«يا أبو صطيف، لازمني سفرة، بس السنة ما رح أعمل متل
ما نصحتني، مرة نصحتني روح عاليونان، ومن بعدا حبلت
أم عبد، ومرة نصحتني روح عباريس وكمان حبلت أم عبد.
سألو أبو صطيف «شو مفكر تعمل يعني؟».
قلو «السنة راح آخد أم عبد معي».

While playing backgammon with Abou Steif one day, Abou Abed said:

"I really need a holiday. But this year, I am going about it a little differently."

In years past, he had always taken Abou Steif's advice on where to go.

"One year, you advised me to go to Greece - I went, and Em Abed got pregnant.

Then a few years ago, you told me to go to Paris - and Em Abed got pregnant again."

"So, what are you going to do differently this time?" asked Abu Steif.

"Well, for starters," Abou Abed announced,

"this year when I go on holiday, I'm going to take Em Abed with me!"

عبد أول مرة بروح على عرس مع أهلو،
تطلع ييو وسألو «ليش العروس لابسي أبيض؟»
قلو «لأنو الابيض لون السعادة واليوم أسعد يوم بحياتا».
سكت شي دقيقة، ورجع سأل بيّو
«طيب ليش العريس لابس أسود؟».

Abed attended a wedding for the first time with his parents.

During the ceremony he turned to his father, and asked,

"Why is the bride dressed in white, *baba?*"

"Because white is the color of happiness, and today is the happiest day of her life,"

replied Abou Abed.

Abed was quiet for a minute and then asked:

"So, then why is the groom wearing black *baba?*"

محامي قنع أبو العبد يكتب وصيتو، بس أول شرط حطّوا أبو العبد كان أنو بعد ما يموت يحرقوه، ويرشّو رمادو بأكبر مجمّع تسوق بيروت.

سألو المحامي «ليش يا أبو العبد؟»

قلّو «لأنو هيك بتأكد أنو أم العبد رح تزورني عا لقليلة كلّ أسبوع مرة».

Abou Abed was advised by a lawyer to draw up his last will and testament.

Abou Abed had two requests:

First, he wanted to be cremated when he died; and second,

he asked for his ashes to be scattered over the largest shopping mall in Beirut.

"Why on earth would you want that?" asked the lawyer.

"Well, that way, I can be sure that Em Abed

will come and visit me every week."

بالليل وعي أبو عبد عا صوت بالصالون،
لما فز من تختو شاف حرامي عم يهرب من
الشباك حامل تلفزيونو الجديد.
صرخ فيه أبو عبد
«عمهلك، رجاع وخود الريموت،
يا أهبل ما بينفعك التلفزيون من دونو».

One night, Abou Abed was woken up by a loud noise
coming from the living room.
He went to investigate, and found a burglar climbing out the window with
Abou Abed's brand-new TV in tow.
"Come back here, you idiot!" shouted Abou Abed.
"You forgot the remote control - the TV won't work without it."

نجح عبد بفحص السواقة وكل العيلة طلعت معو بالسيارة تياخدن مشوار،

طلع أبو عبد ورا إبنو، فقلو عبد «شو مذوق يا بيّي، قعدت ورا حتى تقعّد أمّي حدي وتشوف قديش بسوق منيح؟!»

رّد أبو عبد «قعدت وراك لحتا لبّط فيك من ورا متل ما عملت فيّي سنين».

After Abed passed his driving test, the whole family got into the car
for his first trip as a licensed driver.
Abou Abed headed straight for the back, right behind the driver's seat.
"*Baba*, you are so sweet! You want to sit back there so that mum can sit up front and see
how good a driver I am!" smiled Abed.
"No, no," said Abou Abed. "I want to sit behind you so I can kick the back of your seat while
you drive, just like you've done to me for all these years!"

كان عبد مع أمو بالسوبرماركت لما حس بدوخة،
قلا لأمو «حاسس نفسي عمتقلب»
فقالتلو «روح لبرا وروح ورا الشّجرات تما يشوفك حدا».
ركض عبد ورجع بعد شوي وشكلو أحسن سألتو أمو
«وصلت لورا الشّجرات؟» قلها «لا، ما كان في لزوم لأنو حدّ
الصندوق في علبة مكتوب عليا (مخصص للمرضى)».

Abed was in the supermarket with his mother when he suddenly felt very queasy.

"I think I am going to be sick," he moaned.

"It's ok, *habibi* - run outside and go behind the bushes where no one will see you,"
said his mother.

So, Abed ran for the door and returned just a minute later looking much better.

"Did you make it to the bushes?" asked Em Abed.

"No, *emmi*, I didn't end up having to go outside at all!

I found a box marked, '*For the Sick*' right next to the cashier."

رجع أبو عبد على البيت من لعب الورق متأخّر، ولاقى أم العبد ناطرتو. «وين كنت؟» صرخت فيه. قلها «وطّي صوتك أحسن ما توعّي الجيران»، قالتلو «جاوبني هلّأ، قديش خسرت هالمرة؟» لمح أبو عبد حركة بغرفة النوم وصرخ «شُو عميعمل هالرجّال جوّا؟»
صرخت فيه أم عبد «ما تجرّب تغيّر الموضوع».

As Abou Abed snuck home late from his card game one night,

he found Em Abed waiting up for him.

"Where have you been?" she shouted.

"Shh! Keep your voice down, or you'll wake the neighbors," he said.

"Answer me now! How much did you lose this time?" she demanded.

Suddenly, Abou Abed noticed some movement in the bedroom.

"Hey, what's that guy doing in our bedroom?" he shouted.

Em Abed glared at him and yelled: "Don't you dare try to change the subject!"

لما رجع عبد عالبيت بعد أول يوم بالمدرسة
سألتو أُمّو
«شُو تعلمت بأول يوم؟».
جاوب «الظاهر مش كفاية
لأنو قالولي أرجع بكرا».

When Abed returned home after his first day at school,

his mother asked,

"So, son, what did you learn on your first day?"

Abed replied: "Well, obviously not enough.

They told me that I have to go back again tomorrow!"

اشترى أبو العبد ببغا لأبنو عبد، وأخدو عالبيت وجرّب يعلّمو يقول كم كلمة، بس شو ما قال، يردّ عليه الببغا بمسبّة. آخر شي قبّعت معو وقال للببغا «خلص، رح فرجيك»، قام حطّو بالبرّاد. بعد نص ساعة فتح البرّاد وشال الببغا عم يرجف، قالو الببغا «بحلف ما بقى سبّك، بس خبّرني شو عملت الدجاجة يللي جوا!؟».

Abou Abed decided to surprise Abed with a new pet. So, he went to a pet shop and bought a talking parrot. He brought the bird home and tried to teach it a few words, but instead of repeating them, the parrot just swore at him in the foulest language.

After a few hours, Abou Abed got fed up. "Now, I've had enough of your cursing! As a punishment, I am going to put you in the freezer until you learn your lesson!" Abou Abed shouted. Half an hour later, the parrot cried out, "Please, I beg you, open the door!" So Abou Abed took the shivering parrot out of the freezer. "I will never, ever swear again," the bird promised, "but please, tell me: What did that chicken in the freezer do?"

احترق محل أبو صطيف ببيروت
ولما عرف أبو العبد راح يطمّن عليه،
قلّو «نشكر الله أنت بخير،
بس انشالله ما خسرت كتير بضاعة»؟
قلّو أبو صطيف «مش كل هالقدّ، أغلبية الغراض
بالمحل كان عليها أوكازيون».

After Abou Steif's shop in Beirut was burned down,

Abou Abed called up his old friend.

"Thank God you're safe, *ya zalameh*.

I hope you didn't lose too much in the fire?" he asked, with concern.

"Thank goodness, not that much," replied Abou Steif.

"Most of the merchandise in the shop

was on sale."

أم العبد انحزمت على مؤتمر بجينيف عن حقوق المرأة، لتمثّل النسوان اللبنانيات.
كل مرا حضرت المؤتمر طلبو منها تحمل شي لمّا ترجع عبيتا، الفرنساوية مثلاً، طلبو
منها تبطّل تجلي و تجبر زوجا يجلي. أم العبد طلبوا منها ما بقى تنضّف البيت،
وتخلّي أبو العبد ينضف محلا. بعد سنة رجعو كلّن عجينيف ليخبرو شو صار معن،
قالت الفرنساوية «أول يوم جوزي ما عمل شي، بس تاني يوم غسل فنجانو وشوي
شوي تعوّد يجلي كل يوم». ولما إجا دور أم العبد قالت «أول يوم جوزي ما عمل شي
وكمان تاني يوم ما عمل شي، عجمعة ما حرّك إصبع، بس بعدين شحطني من
البيت وجاب صانعة. وهلق أنا عايشة بالضيعة مع أمي وما معي فرنك، وبدّي
أشكركن على هالنصيحة»

Em Abed was invited to attend an international conference on women's rights. Each woman at the conference was
given a certain task to perform upon returning home. The French woman was asked to stop washing the dishes,
and make her husband do it instead. The Canadian woman was asked to stop cooking dinner, and make her husband
prepare their meals. Em Abed was asked to stop cleaning the house and make her husband do it himself. A year
later, all the women had to report back. "On the first day, my husband did nothing. But on the second day he washed
his own mug, and now he does the washing up every day," said the French woman. "On the first day, my husband
did nothing," recounted the Canadian woman. "But on the second day, he made a sandwich, and now he cooks us
delicious meals every night." Em Abed's turn came. "Well, on the first day my husband did nothing; on the second
day, also nothing; even after a week he had not lifted a finger," she recalled. "But then, finally, he did something!"
The women at the conference smiled at one another and urged her to continue. "Tell us, Em Abed, what did he do?"
"He threw me out of the house and hired a maid. Now I am living back with my nagging mother in the village,
without a penny to my name. So, I'd like to thank all of you for the excellent advice!"

هاجر أبو عبد على أميركا، وفتح تجارة نُرش وثياب داخلية.
بعد ست أشهر اتّصل بأم عبد وقلا «ضبّي غراضك وتعي
لعندي»، استغربت أم عبد وسألتو «شو صار؟»، جاوبا «بعت
100 فرشة و500 قطعة تياب داخلية، وربحت 150 ألف
دولار». ضحكت أم عبد وقالتلو «إي حبيبي لازم أنت تضبّ
غراضك و تجي لهون، أنا على فرشة وحدة، وبلا تياب داخلية
ربحت 200 ألف دولار!».

Abou Abed decided to immigrate to the United States, where he started a small business
selling underwear and mattresses. Six months later, he called Em Abed and told her:
"Pack your bags and come over here!"
Em Abed was surprised, and asked her husband, "What happened?"
"I've sold one hundred mattresses and five hundred sets of underwear, and I've made
$150,000," he replied. Em Abed laughed: "Ha, *la habibi!* In that case, you should pack
your bags and head back here. In the same amount of time, with no underwear and just one
mattress, I've managed to make $200,000!"

مرّة باللّيل بروح أبو عبد وأبو صطيف على الكّازينو. أوّل ما وصّلو بيركض أبو صطيف وبحط ليرة بالمكنة وبتنزلّو قنينة كولا. بصير ينزل ليرة ورا ليرة بها المكنة وتنزلّو قنينة ورا قنينة. وقّف أبو عبد ورا منّو وبلّش صبرو ينفد فحط إيدو على كتف صاحبو «ولك خلّي دور لغيرك ولا ما بدك؟» بيبرم أبو صطيف وبيصرخ «ولك ما شايفا فاتحة معي يا زلمي؟»

One evening, Abou Abed and Abou Steif went to the casino. As soon as they arrived, Abou Steif headed straight for the vending machine. He put in a coin and a bottle of cola popped out. He continued to feed coins into the machine, and the bottles kept popping out.

Abou Abed stood behind him for a while, growing ever more impatient.

Finally, he tapped his friend on the shoulder.

"Let someone else have a go now, will you!" he said.

Abou Steif turned round and shouted:

"*Ya zalameh*, can't you see I'm on a winning streak?"

أبو عبد وأبو صطيف عم يلعبو طاولة زهر بمر واحد من جيران
أبو عبد وبقولو يا عين يا أبو عبد انت قاعد عم تلعب طاولة
ومرتك عم تخونك بالغابة مع أعز أصحابك.بقوم أبوعبد منزعز
وبقول «باطل! أبو صطيف اعذرني بدي قوم شُوف شُو القصة».
بروح أبو عبد و بيرجع بعد خمس دقائق بقولو لأبو صطيف «لعاب
أبو صطيف لعاب... قال عم تخوني قال... أول شي شجرتين ثلاثة
عملي ياهن غابة بعدين هيدا لا صاحبي ولا بعرفو لعاب أبو
صطيف لعاب».

One afternoon, Abou Abed was playing backgammon with Abou Steif when, suddenly, one of his neighbors burst in and said to him: "*Smallah, Smallah!* While you're here playing, your wife is cheating on you with your best friend in the forest!" Abou Abed leapt up and yelled, "No, that's impossible! Excuse me, Abou Steif, but I have to go deal with this!" Five minutes later, Abou Abed returned, rolling his eyes. "Let's get back to the game, the neighbor's story was a total lie," he scoffed. "First of all, that so-called 'forest' was just two or three trees, and secondly, that man is no friend of mine - I don't even know him! Play, Abou Steif, play."

اشترى أبو عبد قنينة عصير من الدكان بس وصل عالبيت لاقى
مكتوب عليها «عصير مركّز».
وصلت أم عبد على البيت بعد ساعة لاقت أبو عبد ماسك
القنينة بإيدو وعم يطلع عليها فسألتو شُو عم يعمل.
جاوبها أبو العبد
«مركّز على القنينة متل ما مكتوب».

Abou Abed bought a bottle of juice from the local shop.

When he got home, he saw that the label read, 'orange concentrate.'

An hour later, Em Abed came home and found him still standing there, with the bottle in his hand, staring at the label.

"What on earth are you doing?" she asked.

"It says 'concentrate,'" he replied.

أم عبد عم تتروق مع أبو عبد، قالتلو
«شفتِ جيراننا الجداد يلي قبالنا قديش معضومين؟
كل يوم الصبح بشوفو عم بيبوسا ويحبطا قبل ما يروح
عالشغل، لي ما بتكون رومنسي متلو؟» تبسم أبو العبد وقال
«ومين قلّك لأ؟ صارلي من أول يوم إجو عالحي بجرّب بوسا،
ما بتخليني وبتفقعني كف».

Em Abed was having breakfast with her husband.

"Have you seen how cute our new neighbors are across the street?"

she sighed. "Every morning, I see him kissing and hugging his wife goodbye.

Why can't you be romantic like that?"

Abou Abed smiled. "Who said I'm not? Since the first day they moved in,

I've been trying to kiss her, but she never lets me

- she always just slaps me across the face."

أبو العبد مخروم بالتكنولوجيا،
لما اشترت مرتو برّاد جديد
صار أبو عبد يسكرو ويفتحو لشي ساعة،
وصل عبد وسأل بيو
«شو عم تعمل يا أبي؟» قلو أبو عبد
«بدّي أعرف من يللي عم يطفي الضو جوا».

Abou Abed has always been fascinated by the latest technology.

So when Em Abed bought a new fridge,

he sat there and kept opening it and closing it for about an hour.

Abed came into the kitchen looking for a snack.

"What are you doing, *baba?*" he asked.

"I'm trying to figure out who keeps on switching off the light inside!"

كان أبو العبد بعطلة بإسبانيا وكان كل يوم يتعشّى بمطعم
حدّ ملعب مصارعة الثيران. وكان يطلب نفس الطبق «بيض
الثور». في نهار، بعد ما طلب أبو عبد طبقو المفضّل بيتفاجأ
كيف البيض أصغر عن العادي. بحيط لصاحب المطعم
وبيسألو عن سبب ها التغيير. برد عليه وبقلو «مرات الثور هو
اللّي بيربح المعركة».

While on holiday in Spain, Abou Abed dined each night at a restaurant next to the bullring.

He always ordered the same dish: the "bull's balls," a regional delicacy.

One day, when Abou Abed's order was served,

he was surprised to find the portion much smaller than usual.

He called the waiter over to ask about the discrepancy.

"Well, sir," the waiter replied,

"Sometimes the bull wins the bullfight."

راح عبد عالسوبرماركت ليشتري أقوى مسحوق غسيل، سألو البيّاع إذا كان عندو غسيل كتير، قلو عبد «لأ، بس بدي غسّل كلبي». رّد البيّاع «بس هيدا كتير قوي وإذا غسلت الكلب فيه رح يموت». ما رد عبد عالبيّاع، اشترى المسحوق وفلّ. بعد كم يوم رجع عبد عالمحل تيشتري شوكولا، سألوا البيّاع عن الكلب، جاوبو عبد أنّو الكلب مات، قالو البيّاع «ما قلتلك ما تستعمل هالمسحوق لتغسلو؟»، تطلّع فيه عبد وقلو «ما مات من المسحوق مات من النشّافة».

One day, Abed went into the supermarket and asked for some extra-strength detergent.

"Do you have a lot of washing to do?" inquired the shop assistant.

"No," Abed replied, "I just need to wash my dog."   "You can't use detergent to wash your dog!" shouted the shop assistant. "It's much too strong - if you wash your dog with this, he'll get sick and die."

But Abed didn't listen, and he bought the detergent anyway. A few days later, Abed returned to the store to buy some chocolate. The shop assistant eyed him warily and asked, "How's the dog?"

"He died," Abed sighed.   "I told you not to use detergent on your dog!" cried the man.

"Actually, I don't think it was the detergent that killed him," replied Abed.

"Well, then what was it?" asked the shop assistant. "I think it was the spin cycle."

راح أبو العبد عند حكيم السنان وقلّو
«يا حكيم ما في لزوم للبنج، بس اقلع لي هالسن»
قلّو الحكيم «يا ريت كل الزبونات قبضايات متلك يا أبو عبد،
دلني عالسن يلي عمبيوجعك؟» صرخ أبو عبد
«فتاح تمك يا عبد وفرجي سنّك للحكيم»

One morning, Abou Abed went to the dentist.

"Now doctor, no need for any anesthetic. Just pull out the tooth!" said Abou Abed.

"If only all my patients were as brave as you are," marveled the dentist.

"Now, tell me, which tooth is hurting you?"

"Abed," called Abou Abed,

"Open your mouth and show him the tooth."

لدفتر السواقة كان لازم أبو عبد طلب،
يكتب فيه عمرو ولون عيونو... لما وصل لخانة «الجنس»
كتب «تلات مرات بالجمعة»،
قلّو الموظف «لا يا أبو عبد، القصد تقول رجال أو مرا»
قلّو أبو عبد «بصراحة، بفضل مرا، بس ما بتفرق».

When Abou Abed went to apply for a driver's license,

he was given a form to fill out with his birth date, eye color, and so forth.

One box on the form was labeled 'sex.' Three times per week, wrote Abou Abed.

"No, no - you should put 'male' or 'female,'" explained the clerk.

"Well, to be honest with you, I do prefer female," admitted Abou Abed.

"But it doesn't really matter... either way!"

نهار كان ماشي أبو عبد عالشط. بقوم بلاقي فانوس قديم. بلّمو وبمسّح
عنو الغبرة. وإذ بيظهر جنّي وبقول «اطلب وتمنى إللي تريدو، إلك بس
أمنية وحدة». بفكّر أبو عبد شوي وبقلو «بدّي تعملي أتوستراد من هون
لقبرص». بيتنهّد الجنّي وبقول «والله هيدا طلب صعب شوي، وما عدت
صغير لكون صريح معك وقوم بالمهمة، فيك تطلب شي تاني معلم؟»
«طيب... لح إطلب غير أمنية»، قرّر أبو عبد. «في شي خصّو بإم العبد...
ما بقدر إفهمها. الصبح بتقوم بمزاج حلو... بس بعدين بتبلّش بتصرّخ
وبيتخربط مزاجها. يا ريت بقدر إفهم عليها!»
بيحبس الجنّي هيك شوي وبرّد عليه «طيب، كم خط بدّك للأتوستراد؟»

While walking along the seafront Corniche one evening, Abou Abed stumbled upon an old lamp. He picked
it up and rubbed it to brush off the dust. Suddenly, a genie popped out. "Your wish is my command," said
the genie. "You may make one wish." Abou Abed thought for a while. "Well, genie, I've decided what I want
from you: I wish for you to build a motorway from here to Cyprus." The genie heaved a great sigh and said:
"That's a pretty tough request I'm not exactly young anymore, and to be honest, I'm not sure I'm up to the
task. Can't you ask for something else, master?" "Well, I could make another wish," agreed Abou Abed.
"It has to do with Em Abed... she really confuses me. In the morning, she'll wake up in a good mood... but
then a moment later, she's in a foul mood and shouting at me. I wish I could understand her behavior!"
The genie frowned and replied: "How many lanes do you want the motorway to have?"

بالصيف راح أبو عبد وأبو صطيف ليزورو لندن. هونيك بيركبو
بياص إلو طابقين. قرّر أبو صطيف يقعد تحت وطلع أبو عبد
لفوق. بعد شويّ وهنّي وبالمشوار، بحيّط أبو عبد لصاحبو «شُو
وين صرتو؟» بردّ عليه أبو صطيف «والله نحنا بعدنا مارقين حد
قصر باكينهام.بقوم بقلو أبو عبد «شكلكن عرفتو تختاروا. نحنا
هون فوق بعدنا ناطرين السواق وبعد ما شرّف حضرتو!»

One summer, Abou Abed and Abou Steif were visiting London.

They boarded a double-decker bus to go to their hotel.

Abou Steif decided to sit below, while Abou Abed headed for the upper level.

Several minutes into the ride, Abou Abed called down to his friend,

"*Shou*, where are you now?"

"We are about to drive past Buckingham Palace," replied Abou Steif.

"I think you made the better choice, my friend," said Abou Abed. "Up here, we're still waiting
for our bus driver - he hasn't even shown up yet!"

عيلة أبو عبد بالضيعا عملت مباراة رماية،
وأخد أبو عبد إبنو محدو ليتفرّج. واحد من قباضايات الضيعا
حطّ تفاحة على راس صاحبو، صوّب عليها وصرخ
«أنا رامبو»، إجا واحد تاني، صوّب وصرخ «أنا جايمس بوند».
قرّب أبو عبد يجرّب حظو، قوّس على التفاحة بس صاب
الرجال وقتلو... فصرخ «أنا آسف!»

One summer, the hunters in Abou Abed's village held a shooting contest,
and Abou Abed decided it would be fun to attend with little Abed.
One of the village's tough guys shot an apple clean off the top of his friend's head,
screaming, "I AM RAMBO!"
Then another guy came along and took a shot, screaming: "I AM JAMES BOND!"
So Abou Abed decided to try his luck and took the gun, aiming at the apple.
But Abou Abed missed and shot the guy in the head... screaming, "I AM SORRY!"

سافر أبو عبد عفرنسا، وصل عباريس بآخر الليل ودغري راح على الكباريه، قلا للمسؤولة «بدّي صبيّة حلوة تبسطني عالطريقة اللبنانية». سألت المدام البنات بس ما حدا كان يعرف الطريقة اللبنانية ولهيك كانوا مترددين، أخيراً وقفت أحلى بنت وقالت «أنا راح أعملو شو ما بدو، بس راح خلّي يدفع ثروة مقابيلا». قضت السهرة مع أبو عبد وبالآخر سألتو «شو هي الطريقة اللبنانية» فقام أبو عبد ودفعلا... بشيك مؤجّل.

Abou Abed took a trip to France. He arrived in Paris late at night and headed straight for a cabaret. "Is there a pretty girl here who will let me enjoy her company 'the Lebanese way'?" he asked the owner of the establishment. The *madame* inquired among the girls if any would be willing. However, no one had ever heard of 'the Lebanese way,' so they were reluctant to say yes. Finally, one of the most beautiful girls at the club summoned her courage and stood up. *I will do whatever it is he wants and I'll make him pay a fortune for it*, she thought, walking towards Abou Abed so, the girl spent the evening with Abou Abed. At the end of the night, she finally asked him: "Tell me, what exactly is 'the Lebanese way'?" Abou Abed got up and paid her... with a post-dated check.

ربح ابو عبد رحلة بالهليكوبتر وأخد أم عبد معه.
بس لما طارو، ما كان يقدر يحكي مرتو أو يدلّ على المناظر
اللبنانية من كتر الضجة،
فقالو للطيرجي
«ولو؟ طفيلنا هالمروحة ما عمنسمع عا بعض،
وأصلاً ما في شّوب اليوم!».

Abou Abed won a sightseeing tour in a helicopter

and decided to bring Em Abed along with him.

But once they took off, Abou Abed found that he couldn't speak to his wife or even point out

the famous Lebanese sites to her over all the noise.

Finally, he shouted out to the pilot: " *Walaw*, can you please turn off the fan?

It's too noisy - and It's not even hot today!"

عرف أبو العبد أنو شركة الكولا بتوزّع جوايز فورية للزبون اللي
بيفتح السدة الربحانة، فاشترى قنّينة وفتحا، لاقى مكتوب عالسدة
«عذراً، حاول مرة أخرى». سكّر القنينة ورجع فتحا ولاقى
«عذراً، حاول مرة أخرى»، ضل يسكّر القنينة ويفتحا كذا مرة،
بالأخير تطلّع بأم عبد وقال
«يلعنن شو كذابين صرت مجرب كذا مرة، شو مفكّريني مجدوب؟».

A soda company was running a promotion that offered instant prizes
with a winning bottle cap. Abou Abed bought a bottle of soda,
twisted off the cap and checked underneath.
It read, 'Please try again!' He put the cap back on the bottle and twisted it off again, but
the cap still said the same thing. He did this over and over before complaining to Em Abed:
"They just keep making false promises and raising my hopes.
Do they think I am stupid, or what?"

من بعد نشرة الأخبار قال أبو عبد
«يا أم عبد، بتعرفي أنو بالهند بيخلق ولد كل ثانيه؟»
قالتلو أم عبد «أنا حظي عاطل بلبنان،
تصّور أني نطرت تسع شهور لخلفت عبد!»

One evening, while listening to the news,

Abou Abed heard something that caught his attention.

He called over to his wife in the next room:

"Em Abed, did you know that a baby is born every second in India?"

"Imagine that!" she cried.

"And to think I had to wait nine months to give birth to Abed here in Lebanon!"

ربح أبو عبد اليناصيب، فعزم أبو صطيف يسافر معو
على جنوب فرنسا ليتصيدو سمك.
رجعو بعد جمعتين وما تصيدو إلا سمكة كبيرة،
قال أبو عبد بتعرف يا أبو صطيف
«هالسمكة كلفتنا 5 ملايين ليرة»، جاوبو أبو صطيف
«منيح ما كمشنا إلا وحدة، إذا كان السمك هلقد غالي».

After winning the lottery, Abou Abed invited Abou Steif to come along
on a fishing trip in the south of France.
When they returned home two weeks later, they had only caught one large fish.
"Well, this fish cost us about five million lira!" remarked Abou Abed.
"It's a good thing we only caught one then," replied Abou Steif,
"since they're so expensive!"

أبو عبد مسرّب وجّ الصبح،
لاقتو أم عبد عالباب وصرخت فيه
«وين كنت؟
في سبب بخلّيك تسرّب عالبيت الساعة ستة الصبح؟»
جاوب أبو عبد
«أكيد، معقولي روّح الترويقة؟».

One night, Abou Abed stayed out very late playing cards with Abou Steif.

When he returned home the next morning, his wife met him angrily at the front door.

"Where have you been?" she shouted.

"There had better be a good reason you're coming home at six in the morning!"

"Of course there is, *habibti*," replied Abou Abed.

"I didn't want to miss breakfast."

فات أبو عبد على بناية أبو صطيف،
شاف ورقة على باب الأسانسور مكتوب عليها
«انتبه للدهان».
فوقف ساعة عالباب،
وبعدين قال «شو هالقصة!
عندي شغل، خلّي غيري ينتبهلو».

Abou Abed was heading into Abou Steif's building
when he noticed a sign on the lift door that read,
'Watch the Paint.'
He stood beside the door for an hour before finally losing patience:
"This is ridiculous! I have work to do
- let someone else come and watch the paint!"

كان أبو عبد ناطر أبو صطيف ليلعبو طاولة زهر،
وإلّا واصل أبو صطيف على موتوسيكل فسألو أبو عبد
«منوين جبت هالموتوسيكل؟» جاوبو أبو صطيف «أنا وجايي
عالطريق، وقفت حدّي بنت راكبة عموتوسيكل وبلشت تشلح
تيابا وقالتلي ´فيك تاخد مّني ياللي بدك ياه´، فأخدت
الموتوسيكل». قلّو أبو عبد
«خير ما عملت، ولا مسكن يزبطو تيابا عليك».

One afternoon, Abou Steif showed up at Abou Abed's house for their game of backgammon on a brand new motorbike. Since his friend usually came on foot, Abou Abed was impressed and asked, "Hey, where did you get that bike from?" "Well, I was walking over, minding my own business, when suddenly a girl pulled up next to me on a motorbike," recounted Abou Steif. "She jumped down and started to take off all her clothes and said, 'You can have anything you want from me!' So I took her bike."

Abou Abed laughed and clapped his friend on the back. "Good choice, my friend... Her clothes would have been much too small for you!"

أبو عبد فات عالبيت، لاقى أم عبد شالحة تيابا بالصالون،
صار يعيِّط ويصرخ فقالتلو أم عبد
«روق ... روق يا أبو عبد،
هول تياب السكس أنا لبستلك ياهن يا حبيبي».
تطلّع فيا أبو عبد وقلا
«طيب كويون شوي!».

Abou Abed returned home one day to find Em Abed lying stark naked
in the middle of the living room.
He quickly became upset, but Em Abed attempted to soothe him, saying,
"These are the clothes of love, *habibi*, and I am wearing them just for you!"
He took a long look at her and replied:
"For goodness' sake, woman - you could at least have ironed them a bit!"

فات أبو عبد عالبيت متحمس وصرخ لأم العبد
«ربحت اللوتو يلّا بسرعة ضبّي غراضك».
أم عبد انبسطت كتير وقالتلو «حبيبي، عظيم كتير،
شو باخد تياب، صيفي للبحر أو شتوي للجبل؟».
جاوبا أبو عبد «ما بتفرق معي ضبّي شو ما بدك،
بس حلي عنّي وأنتِ طالق».

One day, a breathless Abou Abed burst through his front door and shouted out to Em Abed:

"I won the lotto! Quick, pack your bags!"

Em Abed was delighted. She called out, "*Habibi*, that is wonderful news!

Should I pack warm clothes for the mountains or light clothes for the beach?"

"I really don't care, pack whatever you like," Abou Abed replied.

"I just want you out of here as soon as possible so I can celebrate!"

لما عبد بلّش المدرسة صار عند أم العبد وقت فاضي،
فقررت تشتغل بمكتب. بأول يوم شغل وقفت قدام قرّامة الورق
محتارة، شافتا سكرتيرة وشفقت عليا، فأخدت
من إيدا الملف وحطتو بالمكنة،
قالتلا أم العبد «بشكرك، أنا ما بحياتي استعملت مكنة
تصوير، بدّو المدير خمس نسخ إذا سمحتِ».

When Abed started school, Em Abed found that she had a lot of spare time on her hands,
so she decided to take a job in an office. On her first morning,
the receptionist noticed Em Abed standing in front of the shredder, clutching a report,
clearly unsure of how the machine worked.
The receptionist felt sorry for her, and took the report out of her hands
and fed it into the shredder.
"Thank you so much!" said Em Abed, with relief.
"I have never used a photocopier before. The boss needs five copies."

أبو عبد سافر عباريس،
وقعد عند إبن عمو، بس انزعج من الجيران،
قال لأبو صطيف «تصور قديش من مذوقين،
الساعة تلاتي الصبح بيبلشو يدقو عالحيطان وعباب الشقة،
ما بيخلوني إسمع حالي
عمبدق عالدربكة».

Abou Abed took a trip to Paris to visit his cousin.

He loved the city, but was less impressed with his cousin's neighbors.

"They are just so inconsiderate," he told Abou Steif over the phone.

"At three o'clock in the morning, they start banging on the apartment door

and against the walls - they make so much noise that I can barely hear myself

playing the *derbake!*"

«لبنان» إلى جمهورٍ أوسع. قد ينتقد بعضكم اختياري للنكات. ويخيب ظنّه لعدم رؤية نكتته المفضّلة في الكتاب. من يعرف شخصيّة «أبو عبد» يعلم أنّ أفضل نكاته إباحيّة من العيار الثقيل.

برأيي، ينتمي «أبو عبد» إلى حقبة مثاليّة عابرة، لم يواجه فيها اللبناني العاديّ مشاكل كبرى. ولم يكن قلقه الأكبر سوى كيفٍ يتمتّع بوقته مع أصدقائه. يمثّل الرجل اللبنانيّ العاديّ، مع كلّ سيّئاته، لكن أيضاً روعته. وهي روح الفكاهة الفريدة. بالرغم من أنّ قصصه تضحكنا، لطالما تساءلت كيف يمكن «لأبو عبد» المتحيّز الذكوري أن يظهر بطل الطبقة العاملة.

أين هو الآن؟ يبدو أنّ «أبو العبد» أزليّ ويعايش العصور، ويرافق كلّ الأجيال اللبنانيّة. قد لا تكون شخصيّته مثاليّة. لكن ما دامت النكات تتوالى، فما الفرق؟ لنواصل البحث وأخبروني عندما تجدونه، إذ أودّ سماع قصصه منه.

أخيراً وليس آخراً، شكر كبير لباتريك الموهوب والمذهل الذي أحيا شخصيّة أبو عبد وأدخلها القرن الواحد والعشرين.

سابينا، بيروت، كانون الأول ٢٠٠٨
abou-abed@live.com

المقدمة

أبو عبد، مع طربوشه الأحمر وشاربيه الكبيرين، رمز رجولته، هو من أبرز الشخصيّات الفكاهيّة المعروفة في لبنان. تطوّر من كونه نسج الخيال إلى شخصيّة واسعة الصيت. ويتبوّأ مئات النكات. يقضي وقته مع صديقه أبو صطيف في مقهى بيروتيّ، حيث يلعبان الورق وطاولة النرد. وحول فناجين لا تحصى من الشاي، يتبادلان قصصًا مضخّمة تدور عادة حول مآثرهما الجنسّية. ولسوء حاله الماديّة، يلجأ دومًا إلى ألعاب ورق الشدة واليانصيب.

أبو عبد وزّوجته أم عبد لديهما ابنٌ بكر يدعى عبد. يتحمّلان مزحاته لكنهما يثوران من تجاوز حدّه فيقلبان الطاولة عليه. يدفعنا أبو عبد دائمًا إلى التساؤل عن مهنته وميوله الجنسيّة، إذ لا يبدو أنه يمارس أي مهنة. ويرضى بكّل ما يتسّنى له.

أسَرَتني شخصّية «أبو عبد» منذ سنوات عديدة، خلال الحرب الأهليّة اللبنانيّة، التي أرغمت العديد منّا على ملازمة المنزل لفتراتٍ طويلة. قضينا الأمسيات مع الأقارب والجيران، نروي فيها نكات «أبو عبد» لننسى الحال المتوتّرة.

اشتهر زوجي بمجموعة نكاته الواسعة وسرده المسهب. منذ بضع سنوات بدأت أسجّل بعض النكات التي أذكرها. وخطرت لي فكرة نشر كتابٍ يقدّم أحبّ فكاهيي

الى أبو تارا و أبو ويليم

بما أنّ أبو عبد ينتمي إلى المجتمع اللبناني، جزء من عائدات هذا الكتاب ستخصّص لجمعيّة (سيفا) الخيريّة اللبنانيّة لدعم المشاريع الإنمائيّة في أرجاء لبنان.

حقوق النشر محفوظة لسابينا محفوظ

حقوق الرسوم محفوظة لباتريك صفير

حقوق التوزيع الطباعي والتصميم الفنّي لشركة «تورنيغ بوينت»

turning**point**
BOOKS

الطابق 15، بناية كونكورد، شارع دينان، فردان، بيروت، لبنان

ص.ب.   6613 - 14

هاتف: 100 752 1 961+

فاكس: 555 748 1 961+

www.tpbooksonline.com

الطبعة الأولى: كانون الأول 2008 ، الطبعة الثانية: أيار 2009

ISBN: 978-9953-0-0034-4

طباعة:

كتاب نكات أبو عبد

The Abou Abed Joke Book

جمعتها: سابينا محفوظ

رسـوم: باتريك صفير

تنقيح: حمد حيدر، كلود كرم، فيرلي ويلسـون

تصميم: مايا طويل